Angel of the Swamp

DEACONESS HARRIET BEDELL IN THE EVERGLADES

Marya Repko

ECITY • PUBLISHING

Angel of the Swamp; Deaconess Harriet Bedell in the Everglades

Copyright © 2009 text by Marya Repko, All Rights Reserved.

Cover Photo courtesy of Florida State Archives.

Set in Gaudy Old Style, 11/16 pt
Printed and Bound in the U. S. A.

First Edition, Second Printing, September 2022

ISBN 978-097-16006-7-6

ECITY • PUBLISHING

P O Box 5033
Everglades City, FL, 34139
telephone (239) 695-2905
mrepko@earthlink.net

www.ecity-publishing.com

Other books from this publisher:
A Brief History of the Everglades City Area
A Brief History of the Fakahatchee
A Brief History of the Smallwood Store in Chokoloskee, Florida
A Brief History of Sanibel Island
Everglades Entrepreneur; Barron Gift Collier, Roaring Twenties Tycoon
Grandma of the Glades: Marjory Stoneman Douglas
Women in the Everglades; Pioneers and Early Environmentalists
Memories from Hadlyme; A Personal History of the East Haddam, CT, Area
History for Younger Readers:
    The Story of Everglades City
    The Story of Sanibel Island
    The Story of Barron Collier
Oral History as told to Maria Stone:
    The Tamiami Trail; A Collection of Stories
    Ochopee; The Story of the Smallest Post Office

PREFACE

Chokoloskee pioneer C. G. McKinney affectionately referred to mosquitoes as "swamp angels". Patricia Huff, in her Everglades area newsletter *The Mullet Rapper*, coined the phrase "Angel of the Swamp" to praise local people for community involvement. When I was searching for the title of this book, she immediately suggested "Angel of the Swamp" — thank you, Patty, for your generosity.

More of my thanks go to all the friends and neighbors who have contributed their reminiscences of the Deaconess. And, to Bea Frost and Marion Nicolay, who have both studied the life of Harriet Bedell and given presentations about her, for their heartwarming encouragement.

Much of my research has been done via the Internet and I appreciate the help from complete strangers in digging up documents and pictures. In particular, thanks to Meg Smith of the Connecticut Episcopal Diocese, Terry Zinn of the Oklahoma Historical Society, Caroline Atuk-Derrick of the University of Alaska Fairbanks, and Nicole Jackelen of the University of Alaska Anchorage.

Finally, thanks to my proof-readers for finding the silly (and not-so-silly) mistakes. However, the remaining errors are completely mine. I welcome further corrections, comments, and contributions.

Marya Repko
Everglades City, FL
June, 2009

CONTENTS

INTRODUCTION 1

EARLY LIFE, 1875-1907 3

THE OKLAHOMA YEARS, 1907-1916 5

THE ALASKA YEARS, 1916-1931 9

FIRST GLADE CROSS MISSION, 1891-1914 13

COLLIER COUNTY, 1923 17

SECOND GLADE CROSS MISSION, 1933-1960 21

CRAFTS 31

FRIENDS AND NEIGHBORS 35

MARCO ISLAND, 1933-1960 39

CONTROVERSIAL CONCERNS 41

RETIREMENT, 1960-1969 45

RECOGNITION 47

APPENDIX. BRIEF BIOGRAPHIES 51

SOURCES 53

TIME LINE 58

INTRODUCTION

The name of Harriet Mary Bedell, Deaconess, was provisionally added to the list of "Lesser Feasts and Fasts" at the Protestant Episcopal General Convention in 2006. Her canonization on the agenda for the 2009 Convention means that she will be considered to be a "saint".

Three different Indian groups and many other people would agree. Harriet Bedell spent most of her adult life helping individuals without regard for her own welfare. She endured the hardship of primitive transportation and living conditions in Oklahoma, Alaska, and the Everglades, riding on horseback, driving dog sleds, and wading through swamp. She dealt with other languages, learning phrases and modifying her own English to be understood.

She focused on the people she wanted to help and used all her abilities to that end. She was a skilled business woman, negotiating loans and selling merchandise. She was a determined fundraiser, speaking and writing about the needs of her missions. As a teacher, she established schools where pupils of all ages learned to read and write. She also passed on good hygiene practices, often by example. She was a healer of the sick, quelling Tuberculosis outbreaks, coping with influenza epidemics, and bandaging wounds. As a devout church woman, she spread her message among all communities — Indian, white, and black. However, she was a sympathetic listener and understood that not all human beings are the same.

This little book outlines her life and her achievements, especially during her time in the Everglades.

A Deaconess doll crafted by Ann McNichols of Naples in 1997 and sold as a fundraiser for the Museum of the Everglades. *Loaned to the author by Tammy Smallwood, photo by the author.*

EARLY LIFE, 1875-1907

The 1890s was a decade of expansion. The events that took place became the foundation for activities in Harriet Bedell's adult life.

In southern Florida, rail links reached the west coast in 1891 and the lower east coast in 1896. By 1893 the Storter and Smallwood trading posts had been established in Everglades City and Chokoloskee; others were functioning in Fort Lauderdale, Miami, Fort Myers, and Marco Island. In 1891 the Women's National Indian Association started a mission near Immokalee.

In 1892 William Crane Gray was consecrated Bishop of the new Missionary District of Southern Florida.
In 1895 Peter Trimble Rowe was appointed Bishop of the new Alaska Missionary District.
In 1898 Deacon David Pendleton Oakerhater went to the new Whirlwind Mission to the Cheyenne in Oklahoma.

Whilst all this was happening, Harriet Bedell was attending Normal School and beginning her teaching career in Buffalo, New York.

Harriet Mary Bedell was born on March 19, 1875, in Buffalo, New York, to Horace Ira Bedell and Louisa Sophia Oberist Bedell. Her father was a tour boat operator. He lost his prosperity in the economic crash of 1884 and drowned in 1885. Harriet's mother sold their mortgaged house and moved the little family of 3 children to rented accommodations where she took in sewing.

Harriet was confirmed in the Episcopal Church at the age of 12 and graduated from Normal School in 1894. She taught in a one-room school for a year before moving to the Doyle School in

Buffalo. After five years, she was made assistant principal. She also taught Sunday School to the Seneca Indians at a nearby reservation.

During a service at St Mary's-on-the-Hill, she heard a talk by the Reverend Arthur Sherman about his missionary work in China. At the age of 30, Harriet's life underwent a dramatic change. She applied to the Training School for Deaconesses in New York City which she attended in 1906. This was followed by several months in Buffalo at a local hospital where she learned the rudiments of medical treatment.

Her mother objected to having Harriet travel as far as China so a compromise was reached. She would go as a teacher to Oklahoma.

Harriet wrote her "Rules of Life":
1. God is first.
2. Don't worry. Put all in the hands of God. Don't think or talk about troubles.
3. Don't hurry.
4. Don't eat too much or between meals.
5. Don't do two things at the same time.
6. All life involves sacrifice.

THE OKLAHOMA YEARS, 1907-1916

The Whirlwind Mission (named after a recently-deceased chief) had been founded in the Episcopal Missionary District of Oklahoma by Bishop Francis Key Brooke in 1897. After a long trip via Oklahoma City and Watonga, Harriet arrived at the little village of Fay where she was met by David Pendleton Oakerhater (Oak-uh-hat-uh), a Cheyenne warrior who had converted to Christianity while in prison and been ordained as a Deacon.

Harriet was fortunate to have Deacon Oakerhater as her co-worker because he spoke the native language and was anxious that she teach "white ways" so that the Indians could cope in the modern world.

She was given a horse called "Billy" on whom she rode side-saddle to visit outlying allotments. She instituted the practice of having two Indian girls live with her for two weeks to learn about hygiene and the use of cutlery for eating. She also taught them to make muffins, which were a great treat. At Thanksgiving and Christmas, she organized huge feasts after sending letters to benefactors asking for money and food. Her reasoning was that everyone, no matter what culture, understands a feast. There was, of course, a religious ceremony to accompany the banquet and celebration.

Besides her secular teaching, Harriet conducted Sunday School and nursed the sick. Tuberculosis was a common ailment and she tried to break the high fever to save her patients. She was honored when the local Medicine Man gave her his sacred rattle and then joined the Church.

Another honor was to be made a member of the tribe and given the name "Vicsehia" ("bird woman" because she sang as she worked). A special dress was made for her and her hair was braided.

She describes her work in an article published in 1909: [1]

> The school building is old and not large enough for two teachers, but we have to use it for a chapel, school, and all other work we do. We open school with Morning Prayer, each child using a Prayer Book. I then take my twenty little ones to my house, where I convert the sitting room into a schoolroom, which has this advantage, that I am ready to answer any immediate call which may come to the house. There is no doctor within twelve miles, so we have to act as doctors, and nurses, besides being lawyers, amanuenses, and spiritual advisors.

In 1911 Harriet began to lose weight and feel tired. Tuberculosis was diagnosed and she went to Denver for a rest. After attending a healing service there, she was amazed that the next medical test showed her clear of the disease. She considered her recovery to be a genuine miracle.

Her fundraising abilities were proven when enough money was contributed to complete St Luke's chapel on the reservation in 1912. She continued to appeal for donations during speaking engagements on a trip to Buffalo in 1913 and made a great hit when she appeared at her mother's party in Cheyenne dress. She used her education to help write petitions to the Federal government on behalf of the tribe.

Harriet was concerned about the peyote ceremony and eventually attended one. She found that the Indians started with a prayer to the Great Spirit before beating their drums and telling wild stories as the drug took effect. She was so well-respected that

---

[1] "Our Mission to the Cheyennes at Whirlwind, Okla.", *A Round Robin to the Junior Auxiliary*, Church Missions Publishing Co., March 1909, p.17.

a subsequent peyote session stopped when she led in Christmas carol singing through the village.

In 1915 the Indians were encouraged to return to their allotments rather than camping out near the Mission while their children were at school. The children were sent to boarding schools and plans were made to close the Mission. When Harriet went to New York on leave in 1916 she was told that she was being transferred to Alaska where her teaching skill with Native Americans was needed.

Harriet (right) in her special dress and braided hair at the Whirlwind Mission. *Photo Courtesy of Oklahoma Historical Society.*

Picture of Stevens Village taken by Archdeacon Hudson Stuck showing the school house near the flagpole. *Photo Courtesy of Frederick John Date papers, Archives and Special Collections, Consortium Library, University of Alaska Anchorage.*

A clipping of Bishop Rowe in Stevens Village. *Picture Courtesy of Walter and Lillian Phillips Collection, UAF-1985-72-46, Archives, University of Alaska Fairbanks.*

THE ALASKA YEARS, 1916-1931

Harriet regretted not being able to return to "her Indians" but started out on a month-long journey to Alaska by train and boat. When she arrived at Juneau she was met by Bishop Peter Trimble Rowe and sent on to Nenana, west of Fairbanks. There she found a relatively civilized community at St Mark's mission with a resident school nurse, a housemother for the boarders, and a local priest.

In fact, it was too civilized. She requested a transfer to a more remote location and was assigned to Stevens Village which she had glimpsed on her boat trip the previous year. As she settled in for the winter, she realized that there would be no communication with the outside world until the "break up" of the ice on the river many months later — unless one traveled by dog sled. This was the next mode of transportation that she learned to use, as well as walking around on snow shoes. The following spring she planted a garden so that she could bottle vegetables for the winter.

Again, she invited two young girls to stay with her for a few weeks at a time to learn about white customs. She nursed the sickly and bandaged up wounds. There were Christmas festivities which included prayer, a decorated tree, gifts, and food. She baked bread once a week, letting it freeze naturally in the -40°F weather and taking a loaf into her wooden cabin to defrost as it was needed.

Harriet showed spunk when she broke up a drunken party funded by the hunters' profits and dragged the younger boys back to the mission. The Chief commended her because he had expressed a desire to stop the drinking and gambling in the little town.

In September, 1922, she went "outside" on furlough to the 47th General Convention in Portland, Oregon, where she was "set apart" as a deaconess. She traveled to Buffalo to see her family and give talks to raise money, staying until June 1923. On her return to Alaska, there was a celebration to welcome her back but some of the smaller children were shy of her new head covering.

Life was difficult for the natives because the fish stocks were being depleted for the canneries. Harriet suggested to Bishop Rowe that a boarding school be established so that the parents could leave to hunt and fish. In 1926 she was again on furlough, speaking and raising money for a "Memorial Fund" that would be used for the boarding school. When she returned, she took the girls into her own house and had a wing built onto the mission for the boys; thus she had to take care of the children as well as teach them. She was also tending the sick and dealing with outbreaks of influenza.

It was decided that the boarding school could be relocated to the old hospital in Tanana. The log buildings at Stevens Village were disassembled and floated down the river; Harriet slept in a tent on the raft behind the boat and cooked for the workers. Bishop Rowe Hall, as the new boarding facility was called, was finally finished but donations were meager after the Wall Street stock market crash in October, 1929.

In September 1931, Harriet left again for a trip to Buffalo but, despite her many speeches, there were few donations. Fortunately, the Diocese of Western New York agreed to pay the $2,200 debt that was owed to Tanana traders. But, there was no money to reopen the boarding hostel and no need for Harriet to return to Alaska.

Hudson Stuck, Archdeacon of the Yukon (and himself an intrepid explorer who climbed "Denali", Mt. McKinley) wrote in 1920, just before he died: [1]

> Miss Harriet Bedell, of long experience in Indian work ... for three years past has lived all alone in the village ... one of the most isolated spots in interior Alaska ... Such a post requires a missionary entirely absorbed and happy in the work, and such a one is Miss Bedell.

---

[1] Stuck, Hudson, *The Alaskan Missions of the Episcopal Church*, Domestic and Foreign Missionary Society, New York, NY, 1920, p.138.

Indian canoes at the Storter trading post in the town of Everglade. *Sketch from the Storter Collection, Courtesy of Collier County Museums, Naples, Florida.*

Josie Billie and Frank Brown, son of the Boat Landing owner, in 1908. Josie is wearing a hat, vest, and tie from the trading post. Frank was later an Indian agent. *Photo Courtesy of Florida State Archives.*

FIRST GLADE CROSS MISSION, 1891-1914

Florida was made a state in 1845 and acquired all the "swamp and overflowed land" at the southern end of the peninsula in 1850.

In the late 1800s, South Florida was mainly an uninhabited wilderness of swamp land and dense jungle. Key West was an exception — it was a booming shipping port, seat of vast Monroe County, and had a thriving Episcopal congregation at St Paul's.

Some Indians had fled into the area to avoid being deported to reservations in the west and had established camps in the Big Cypress and Everglades. The last of the Seminole War battles took place in the Big Cypress in 1857 and the Indians remained. The Platt Report in 1879 recommended providing land for them in Florida rather than trying to remove them.

White settlers had begun to arrive; small clusters of pioneers cropped up on both coasts near the old forts (eg, Ft Lauderdale, Ft Dallas, and Ft Myers). By the 1890s there were trading posts scattered about; Storter in Everglade, Smallwood in Chokoloskee, Collier in Marco, Stranahan in Ft Lauderdale. Indians came with their pelts and plumes which they sold to buy supplies and ammunition.

There was concern about the Indians. The Seminoles in the south were independent and inclined to be nomadic, moving camps to be near good hunting grounds. As white farmers pushed further inland, the Indians were displaced from the land they traditionally used. Drainage of the Glades, begun in the 1880s by Hamilton Disston and continued by Governor Napoleon Bonaparte Broward in 1906, changed the landscape and the distribution of wildlife.

The Seminoles had a profound distrust of the whites, especially anyone associated with the Government which had fought to relocate them. The sordid betrayals by officialdom of Billy Bowlegs and Osceola were still part of Indian memory.

The Indians were, however, reported to be "industrious and self-supporting"[1]. Traders like Ted Smallwood learned to communicate in the Hitchiti language and some of the Indians picked up enough English to cope. Another reason for distrusting whites was the treatment they received from itinerant peddlers who would cheat them out of their furs and sell them inferior whiskey. They were pleased to find honest, sympathetic trading posts.

In 1891 the Women's National Indian Association (WNIA), under the leadership of its president Mrs Amelia Quinton, made an arduous foray with Capt F. A. Hendry into the hinterland. The Association bought 400 acres about 45 miles southeast of Fort Myers, near Lake Trafford, and started a mission. Dr and Mrs J. E. Brecht arrived to take charge. The Government bought 80 acres to set up a sawmill with the hope that the Indians would learn modern techniques while more buildings were constructed. It was found that the Seminole men liked the machinery and were handy with tools. Mrs Brecht taught the Indians to eat with a knife and fork. She observed that the Indians were less shy after a meal. There were big celebrations on July 4th with fireworks when the Indians would camp near the mission.

The Protestant Episcopal Diocese of Florida found it difficult to cover the undeveloped territory in the South. In 1892 it split and formed the Missionary District of Southern Florida under the leadership of Bishop William Crane Gray. An imposing figure

---

[1] Coe, *Red Patriots*, p.225.

with a flowing beard in later life, Gray had a passion for missions and traveled from his headquarters in Orlando in extreme conditions to visit the settlements under his jurisdiction. He would use any means of transportation available: rail, steamship, oxcart, canoe, or horse.

In 1894 the Church took over the WNIA mission. Bishop Gray called the place Immokalee, the Indian word for "home", and built Christ Church over which the Reverend Henry Gibbs presided. However, the Indians did not come to the mission as much as had been hoped so the Bishop decided to take the mission to them.

The Glade Cross Mission was established in 1898 some 30 miles further into the interior, near the trading post at Brown's Landing which was on the canoe trails. A large beam tied to a tree served as its symbol. Rev and Mrs Gibbs spent much of their time here until 1905 when Dr W. J. Godden, a British pharmacist, took their place. Godden treated the sick and dealt with a measles epidemic, housing and feeding his patients until they recovered. In 1908 Bill Brown sold his trading post to the Mission and Dr Godden converted it into a chapel after he had built a new store and hospital. He was helped in his religious work by the Reverend Irenaeus Trout who traveled from Fort Myers to give the sacraments. Dr Godden himself was ordained in 1912.

Bishop Gray announced his retirement at the end of 1913 and Dr Godden died suddenly in 1914. The mission was closed for lack of converts.

Barron Collier (center) on a rail cart at the Deep Lake citrus farm.
Photo Courtesy of Collier County Museums, Naples, Florida.

The town of Everglades in 1928: aerial photo looking west toward the river and bay. The Mission house would be about a mile to the north.
Photo Courtesy of Collier County Museums, Naples, Florida.

COLLIER COUNTY, 1923

By 1920 the remote little village of Everglade was a thriving agricultural center. The river afforded good access by water and produce was shipped to Key West or Ft Myers. Farming was spread all around the area, in the Ten Thousand Islands and at Halfway Creek, as well as in the town. Sports fishermen visited, staying in the large home of pioneer George Storter, Jr (now the Rod & Gun Lodge and Restaurant).

A large citrus farm had been planted 13 miles north at Deep Lake and tracks had been laid from the packing shed to the river so that the fruit could be moved on primitive rail carts for onward shipping. Further afield, there were two villages on Marco Island. At Immokalee, Bill Brown had started the first store after his departure from the Landing and the Roberts family began ranching in 1914, raising cattle for beef.

Most of the area was now part of Lee County which had been cut out of Monroe County in 1887. The County seat was the prosperous town of Ft Myers, winter home of Thomas Alva Edison and Henry Ford.

Unfortunately, the County Commissioners did not see much past their own doorsteps and had no concern for the lack of facilities in the bottom of their jurisdiction. Schools had been financed but roads were almost non-existent. There was no bridge to Marco Island, a cause for which pioneer Tommie Stephens Barfield (the "Queen of Marco") petitioned relentlessly.

Into this frontier came Barron Gift Collier, a Tennessee native who had made his millions at an early age from streetcar advertising. In 1911 he visited business associate John Roach on the island of Useppa, off the coast of Ft Myers, and "got sand in his shoes". Collier bought the island and turned it into a first-class resort. After visiting the grapefruit farm at Deep Lake, he bought that. The buying spree did not stop until 1922 when he owned almost 1 million of acres in Southwest Florida.

Most of Collier's property was undeveloped and inaccessible. The "Tamiami" Trail, a road from Tampa on the west coast to Miami on the east, had been started before World War I but work stopped when Lee County could not raise funds for construction through its territory.

With persuasive lobbying to the State legislation in Tallahassee by Tommie Barfield, Collier's land holdings were split off into a new county named after him. He guaranteed to finish the road.

Collier selected the town of Everglade (which he renamed "Everglades") as his headquarters and county seat because it was central and had good shipping access. He hired David Graham Copeland, an engineer with a Naval background, to supervise operations. The town was neatly laid out, a bank and courthouse built, housing for workers supplied, and engineering facilities developed for the Trail construction.

It took five years to complete the road. Large dredges dug up fill for the roadbed, creating parallel "borrow" canals. The local Indians helped to plot the course and clear brush. They also worked on the road north to Immokalee and the adjacent railroad.

The Trail opened up the area for settlement. Tomato farming began in Ochopee and Copeland and tourists drove past previously-unseen landscape. But, the road changed the Indians' traditional habitat; water stopped flowing to the south of the road. Several years later, the Hoover Dike around Lake Okeechobee and sugar cultivation further altered the Glades ecology. As more land was despoiled or developed, both animals and Native Americans found themselves squeezed out

Collier County, 1923

This picture of Indians picking tomatoes near Ochopee is from the Bedell Collection. *Photo Courtesy of Florida State Archives.*

A postcard of the Tamiami Trail showing the Trailways bus stopping across from an Indian village on the canal. *Photo Courtesy of Florida State Archives.*

The Deaconess and visitors outside the Glade Cross Mission in the town of Everglades. *Photo Courtesy of Florida State Archives.*

The Deaconess welcomed youngsters inside the Mission and in her garden. *Photos Courtesy of Florida State Archives.*

SECOND GLADE CROSS MISSION, 1933-1960

Harriet, still hankering for Alaska, went to New York City in 1931 and worked in the slums when not speaking to raise money. Some variety came when she was asked to talk in Florida early in 1933. After a presentation in Miami, she was invited to visit a Seminole village. What she found was an orchestrated show piece with Indians acting out what was thought visitors wanted to see – fake marriages and alligator wrestling. There were two such places in Miami, Musa Isle and Coppinger's, both of which had started up when the Florida tourism and real estate boom had taken off.

Harriet was appalled at the indignity of it all. She was not the only one; James L. Glynn, Special Commissioner to the Florida Seminoles, wondered about how these children would grow up when "the only home some of [them] have is the cynosure of exhibition and sensation".[1]

While still in Miami she learned what she could about the elusive "Trail Indians" and the long-closed Glade Cross Mission. She approached Bishop Wing of the South Florida Diocese. He put up some practical objections (money, transportation) that she optimistically did not think would be an impediment to her goal. She returned to the New York slums and started a letter-writing campaign. The Bishop eventually granted her $50/month above her salary to return to Florida and open a mission. Glynn, who had been pastor at the Everglades church before taking up his position with the Seminoles, arranged for her move to the town.

---

[1] Glynn, *My Work among the Florida Seminoles*, p.104.

Harriet's new Mission building was a 4-room cottage with a central hallway, called "shotgun" house because you could stand at the front door and shoot a gun out the back door. It was on the main road into town and visible from the railroad. The house, like all of them in Everglades, was owned by the Collier Company. The rent was $20/month. Before she settled, manager D. G. Copeland agreed to paint the inside and find some furniture for her.

The town was run like a ship, orderly and with a command structure. The Collier interests controlled everything but were benevolent. There was a whistle in the morning to begin work, others to announce the lunch break start and finish, and one at the end of the work day. The grass was mowed and flowerbeds kept tidy. Collier's Manhattan Mercantile stores accepted "scrip" (called "boogie books" by locals), the company's own money in which workers were paid. There were black and white schools, a black church, and a white Presbyterian congregation that met at the Community Center. At the exclusive Rod & Gun Club, the Bavarian chef "Snooky" presided and welcomed famous guests. Collier himself would arrive on his yacht for meetings and meals. The laundry cleaned all the company linens, the bank also housed the newspaper office, and the post office contained the telephone exchange.

Harriet's biographers William and Ellen Hartley describe it as: [2]

> A graciously arranged midget city ... almost as if a modern city ... had been dropped into the middle of a South American jungle. But a fisherman, naked to the waist and barefoot, was plodding amiably through one of the downtown streets and growling a greeting to a man in exquisitely tailored clothes.

---

[2] Hartley, *A Woman Set Apart*, pp. 212-213.

One of the first people Harriet got to know was Dr Pender who operated the 5-bed hospital with his wife Laura, a trained nurse, and was allowed to treat the Indians.

It took patience but eventually she contacted an Indian in the town and told him of her willingness to buy Seminole crafts for resale.

In the "Southern Churchman" on February 9, 1935, she wrote:[3]

> Christmas, 1934, was a most joyous occasion among the Seminole Indians in South Florida. In 1933 they came to the Mission in a suspicious manner, but they all enjoyed the feast and listened very attentively to the story of Jesus' Birth. When we asked them if they had a good time, some of the young men said, "Next time more come."
>
> This year, long before Christmas, the Indians began asking, "How long Christmas?" And several days before the celebration, they began to gather in Everglades. At last the Day came. The men put up the Tree, and the children had great fun throwing the tinsel over the branches. Then the gifts provided by Church friends were piled under the Tree. The women did the cooking on an open fire. We had beef, macaroni and tomatoes, rice, coffee, bread. Mr. Copeland, in charge of the Collier interests in Collier County, donated oranges, and the Woman's Club of Everglades and friends provided the candy.
>
> I wish all who helped to make our Christmas such a joyous one could realize what their partnership means to me. I am welcome in all the villages now and never have any difficulty in assembling them together for prayer and the Gospel Story. I expect

---

[3] *Florida Writers' Project Digital Collection*, Carl S. Swisher Library at Jacksonville University, http://voyager.ju.edu/ju-images/cdcorse/ccj506/cc506p.html.

soon to have the girls live with me - two, for two weeks at a time - as I did in Oklahoma and Alaska.

The Deaconess visited camps along the Trail and further inland, telling the story of Jesus and going about her secular tasks: teaching hygiene and healing the sick. She tried to get the Indians to use individual bowls and spoons (rather than eating out of a central pot) so that the colds they picked up while shopping in white stores did not spread throughout the camp. She also encouraged them to bury their trash. Mission camps were set up outside the city so that she could stay overnight and minister to whole families of Indians at the same time. A chickee was built near Immokalee to take care of the sick.

In a Report to Bishop Wing, she wrote:[4]

> Two years have passed since starting work among the Seminole Indians. They soon learned that the Church was their friend ...
>
> Hardly a day passes that the Indians do not come to Everglades. They come to trade at the stores and assemble in the village made for them by the Collier Company. They always stop at the Mission and are now coming in a natural and friendly way.
>
> During the summer travel in the Glades is very difficult - water, water, everywhere. The Indians have built their villages on high ground - little oasis [sic] scattered through the Glades. To get to them we often must go through from four to nine inches of water. Sometimes our Indian driver says "We walk now." This means taking off our shoes and stockings and proceeding through the watery trails. When water reaches the fenders and the trails are

---

[4] *Florida Writers' Project Digital Collection*, Carl S. Swisher Library at Jacksonville University, http://voyager.ju.edu/ju-images/cdcorse/ccj57/cc57b.html.

too soft, we sometimes go in a canoe. You forget all discomforts, however, as you sit in a canoe and glide through the tall grass, the Indian standing and paddling at one end.

The industrial work has developed rapidly. We do not teach them how to make the articles they bring in, but just suggest that they try to make baskets, etc., from the grass growing around them, and encourage them to improve the workmanship of the palmetto baskets, which they have been making for a long time. We also insist that they put their best work into what they do. They have much innate talent for carving and are making plaques, bookends, and dolls.

The Indians are very poor ... they come to the Mission for help, many times saying they have nothing to eat, but they always bring articles they make for me to buy, never coming to beg. I have become overstocked and there being no market during the summer, the gift and souvenir shops being closed for the season, it is difficult to dispose of the things. We are working hard to find a market and will appreciate the help of our friends.

The Indians still remember Bishop Gray ... one of the men to be baptized lived with Dr. Godden when he was a little boy.

Our dwelling in Immokalee is finished but we need equipment - pump for water, etc. A short time ago we spent the night there. We sang and had evening prayer and when we were ready to retire for the night, two young women came in and without saying anything made their bed in the big room. They could not talk English and one of the men said, "So you not be lonesome." They are always very thoughtful and extend many little courteous attentions when we are among them.

> Our days are very full and it is so impossible to work at letters.
>
> The care of the sick is an important part of our work. They send for us or bring their sick ones to the mission. Dr. Pender of the Collier Hospital here is ever ready to treat them. In the glades visits we often find medicine-men caring for the sick. At first they were not friendly but going as we do with Indians they saw we wanted to help.

The Deaconess negotiated revolving loans from the Collier Corporation. They would give her up to $500 in "scrip" which she used to pay the Indians for their crafts. They would take the money to the company stores for food and materials. After she had sold the Indian souvenirs, she paid back the loan.

When an influenza epidemic broke out in 1937 and the little local hospital was full, she took the sufferers into her own home where she feed them soup and aspirin. Her efforts were appreciated by the Medicine Man who called her "sister". She was also known as "in-co-shopie", the woman of God.

The Deaconess became such a respected figure among the Trail Indians that the Collier County Sheriff asked her to visit a camp to discipline a teen who had misbehaved after drinking too much beer. When State and Federal officials wanted to meet with the Indians, the only neutral territory for the conference was the Glade Cross Mission.

Bea Frost, who lectured about the Deaconess as a volunteer with the Friends of the Museum of the Everglades in the 1990s, said that she met a Seminole and asked if he knew the Deaconess. The reply was "yes, and I loved her." Then, according to Frost, he pointed to the heavens and said "she knew God."[5]

---

[5] Script for a talk given by Bea Frost, 1998.

In 1943 Harriet Bedell had reached the mandatory retirement age of 68. There was no question in her mind, of course, of giving up her work. Her salary was replaced by a pension and she was assigned as the "parochial missionary" to St. Stephen's Church in Coconut Grove. In 1948 the Mission House was given to the church by the Collier Corporation.

Marjory Stoneman Douglas, whose 1947 book *Everglades: River of Grass* is a history, as well as a plea for conservation, thanks the Deaconess for her help and for transportation. Describing their visits to the Trail Indians, Douglas wrote:[6]

> The deaconess, like a small steam engine in dark-blue petticoats, walks fast in and out of the trail camps, speaking to everybody by name, asking about sick babies, bringing some old man a mattress pad for his aching bones, trying to get them to use and scald individual drinking cups, scolding a man after a long drunk, taking somebody to the hospital, or getting work for the boys. But her most valuable work has been the improvement of their handicrafts. She has built up for them a profitable trade in Indian dolls and baskets and Indian shirts and skirts.
>
> The deaconess has been asked sometimes by the trail Indians to take part in some funeral of theirs in the deep Glades. When [the Indian ceremony] is over someone nudges the deaconess and says, "Now you begin," knowing well that the sincere prayer of a friend does no harm.

---

[6] Douglas, *Everglades; River of Grass*, pp. 288-289.

The Deaconess tried to go everywhere in her car and sometimes needed a bit of help from her friends. *Photos Courtesy of Florida State Archives.*

The Deaconess wrote on this picture in 1935 "Some places my car cannot go". *Photo Courtesy of Florida State Archives.*

When she finally did arrive, she was assured of a warm welcome. *Photo Courtesy of Florida State Archives.*

Seminole women sewing patchwork with hand-operated machines. *Photo Courtesy of Florida State Archives.*

The Deaconess looking at one of the baskets that has been brought to the Mission. *Photo Courtesy of Florida State Archives.*

CRAFTS

The practice of sewing and using a variety of colors in each garment dates back long before the 1930s. Ted Smallwood kept bolts of calico for his Seminole customers. Mrs Frank Stranahan had a hand-cranked sewing machine that could be used by the women. At the first Glade Cross Mission the Reverend Trout had plans in 1907 to purchase "...10 to 15 sewing machines, where the squaws may come to do their sewing, and to provide instruction in the use of same."[1]

It is thought that patterned material became scarce during World War I (1914-1918) because the dyes came from Germany so styles changed and bits of solid-colored material were sewn together to give variety.

The main products made for and sold by the Glade Cross Mission were carvings, patchwork, baskets, and dolls. The skills and materials were used variously in the products. For example, dolls with wooden and/or palmetto bodies had patchwork costumes. Some baskets had dolls' heads on the lids as knobs.

The carving was done by the men and included models of boats as well as doll bodies. The patchwork and basketry was the province of the women.

Barbour quotes the Deaconess as saying about dolls:[2]
> One day some friends of mine asked why they did not make hands and feet on the women. An Indian girl replied, "Indian woman no show her feet, no show her hands, and we no make 'em". The old men are adept with the knife and are used to carving models of their dugout canoes and are beginning to make carved bowls, bag handles, napkin rings, book ends, and even carved busts which are quite good replicas of themselves.

---

[1] Covington James W., "The Seminole Indians in 1908", *Florida Anthropologist*, Sept 1973, p.101.

[2] Barbour, *That Vanishing Eden*, p.54.

Deaconess Bedell suggested other objects that would appeal to the tourist but could be made with traditional motifs: potholders, aprons, cushion covers. She also introduced coiled baskets made from sweet grass, sewn with colored thread, in all shapes and sizes. However, she rejected items that were not native such as tomahawks and totem poles.

Seven patchwork patterns were selected and named by the Deaconess, giving the Mission a "house style" that could be recognized. Rickrack was forbidden as not authentic.

The Deaconess classified the crafts activity as "Industrial Work" and approached it professionally. She controlled the quality strictly and turned her determination towards marketing, even traveling as far as New York, her car filled with merchandise. She also conducted a lively mail-order business from the Mission and welcomed visitors to Everglades. The spare room in the shotgun cottage was devoted to storage and even her own bedroom was piled up with goods.

Historian Doris Reynolds recalls: [3]
> Although the Chamber of Commerce office in Naples was small and cramped, Harriet would regularly bring Seminole Indian crafts to be sold. No amount of cajoling would dissuade her, and I finally made room for them.

Wilfred Neill, writing in 1956, says: [4]
> Today the Seminoles bring the best and most representative items of their handicraft to Deaconess Bedell, who soon locates a buyer. It would be better to say that the buyers come to Deaconess Bedell; even professional anthropologists, seeking to round out their collections of genuine Indian craftwork, make their way to Glade Cross Mission. The project not only brings financial aid to the Seminoles, but also makes them feel that their arts and crafts are truly worthwhile.

---

[3] Reynolds, *When Peacocks Were Roasted*, p.144.

[4] Neill, *The Story of Florida's Seminole Indians*, p.89.

Patsy West, in her 1984 article, sums it up:[5]

A large percentage of the arts and crafts selling today in the Seminole marketplace reflect Bedell's innovations. The influence of Glade Cross Mission and Deaconess Harriet M. Bedell is, and will continue to be, an indelible part of Seminole and Miccosukee arts and crafts.

A covered basket with a doll head and a sifting basket. *Photo Courtesy of Florida State Archives.*

---

[5] West, "Glade Cross Mission", *American Indian Art Magazine*, Autumn 1984, p.67.

The Deaconess in her sitting room at the Glade Cross Mission. The "money tree" was given to her by neighbors and had 85 dimes to celebrate her 85th birthday. *Photo Courtesy of Florida State Archives.*

The Deaconess in her garden at the rear of the Mission; the log shed at the right is the "snail house". *Photo Courtesy of Florida State Archives.*

FRIENDS AND NEIGHBORS, 1933-1960

As if taking care of the Indians were not enough, the Deaconess participated in local activities and ministered to groups around town and in Marco Island. She went to PTA meetings, gave invocations and talks, was present at baby showers, and attended the Women's Auxiliary at the local Community Church. In 1939 she was listed as a representative for Everglades on the Collier County board of health. She held services at the local jail. She visited the sawmills and remote white families.

She kept up her garden behind the Mission which had a small shed devoted to her snail collection. When she was not writing letters, she knitted afghans which she sold to raise money for the Mission.

During the more than 25 years that the Deaconess spent in Everglades City, she got to know several generations of people and they, in turn, have remembrances of her.

Everyone commented on her driving. Apparently, she slammed her foot down on the accelerator until the car got up to about 45 mph, then took her foot off until it slowed down to around 20 mph which was time for another assault on the gas pedal. This practice resulted in traffic jams on the Tamiami Trail but locals could guess who was at the head of the line. It was also said that she would go around the traffic circle at the center of Everglades City whichever way was shorter.

Arita Hoffman Parker said that she and her sister lived only a block away from the Mission. When their father, the City electrician, asked "What are you doing today, Deaconess?" the answer would be "God Work". He is reported as saying "I work with electricity and that can be dangerous, but meeting the Deaconess in her Model A can be more dangerous."[1] Arita added that if she misbehaved, the threat was "we'll send you to the Deaconess" and if her grades were bad, the Deaconess would give her books to read and report on.[2]

The Deaconess impressed the local children. One of them, now grown up, wrote that "the inside of the Mission was the first time in my life I had seen books in a home and I have had them in my home ever since." Other memories are that "she was always smiling" and "she was a little bitty thing".[3] Still others remember going to the Mission after school for cookies but having to leave if the Indians arrived to do business.

She persevered until she got her way. George Huntoon, an executive at the Collier Development Corporation and later president of the Collier County Historical Society, recalled that she would come tromping up the stairs to his second floor office in the old Everglades Inn to request help. In an attempt to avoid these confrontations, his secretary would say that he was not in while he snuck down the fire escape. It did not take long for the Deaconess to realize the ruse and meet him at the bottom of the steps. He wrote in 1989, "I had many experiences with Deaconess Bedell. She worked principally with the Seminole Indians and did remarkable things to help them. When the Deaconess got after you for something, I found it was best to acquiesce and comply with her request because she would keep after you until you got it done for her."[4]

---

[1] Script for a talk given by Bea Frost, 1998.

[2] Notes from a Story-Telling event, Friends of the Museum of the Everglades, April 22, 2006.

[3] private communication by email, 5/16/09.

[4] Huntoon, "Memories and Tall Tales of Collier County", *The Timepiece*, p.13.

After years of eating canned food in remote Oklahoma and Alaska, the Deaconess kept up the practice. Inez Magill remembers being invited for a meal of canned carrots, canned meat, canned fruit, and instant coffee. When Magill returned the hospitality with a home-cooked meal, she remarked, "The Deaconess doesn't like to cook, but sure does like to eat."[5]

Magill also wrote, "The Deaconess was as naive as a child, but kindly and cordial to all who stopped at her place, which was just at the edge of town. She was an easy victim to a hard luck story."[6]

Naturalist Thomas Barbour wrote in 1944:[7]

> Miss Bedell, whom I have known for years, is a hard-boiled realist. She has helped the Indians get medical care, and has taught them a lot about personal and camp hygiene, and child care. She has encouraged them to do better work at wood carving, basketry, and the manufacture of other objects of various sorts, which she has sold for their benefit.

Just as this book was being finalized a descendent of the Brown family, who had operated the trading post at the Landing, said that the original Glade Cross Mission bell was moved by the family to their restaurant in Immokalee where it was rung on special occasions. The bell was finally given to the Deaconess who donated it to the Everglades Community Church. It peals sonorously every Sunday at 10:55 a.m. to call people to worship in Everglades City.[8]

---

[5] Magill, *From Ticks to Politics*, p.36.

[6] Magill, *From Ticks to Politics*, p.3.

[7] Barbour, *That Vanishing Eden*, p.52.

[8] private communication, Everglades Community Church, May 25, 2009.

The Deaconess outside the Mission of Our Saviour on Marco Island. *Photo Courtesy of Florida State Archives.*

The Deaconess on the porch of the Mission of Our Saviour after it was moved to Goodland. *Photo Courtesy of Florida State Archives.*

MARCO ISLAND, 1933-1960

Marco Island, about 30 miles to the west of Everglades City, is the largest and northernmost of the Ten Thousand Islands. It is famous for the archeological artifacts of the ancient Calusa Indians who inhabited the southwest coast when the Spanish explored in the 1500s. The natives were responsible for the shell mounds which provide the only high ground in the islands and for some remarkable man-made canals. They eventually disappeared after contracting European diseases or, possibly, moving to Cuba.

By the 1930s there were two villages on the island. The founding family in Marco village at the north end of the island was descended from W. T. Collier who arrived with 8 of his 12 children in 1870. His son Captain W. D. ("Bill") Collier ran the trading post and was a leading citizen. Although this Collier family were also from Tennessee, they were not related to Barron Gift Collier.

The Stephens and Barfield families occupied Caxambas to the south while pineapple farming took place in the middle. Tommie Stephens Barfield helped Barron Collier to buy most of the island in 1922 and to persuade the Florida legislature to create Collier County in 1923.

There were two clam factories on the island that processed the phenomenal harvest dredged up in the Gulf.

The Deaconess was active here soon after she arrived in Everglades. She held sewing classes and taught Sunday School at the little "Mission of Our Saviour" in the village of Caxambas. She rented part of a cottage so she could stay overnight. She was helped in her medical work by a nurse who was the wife of a local fisherman.

When one of her students later got married, the Deaconess arranged for a minister to come from Ft Myers to perform the service and bought the couple a marriage license as their present.

In 1948 the Collier Corporation moved all the houses in Caxambas to nearby Goodland so that they could develop the island. They donated a new site to the Mission and arranged to have the building moved.

The buildings were seriously damaged during Hurricane Donna in 1960. In 1964 the Deltona Company, who were developing Marco Island, gave land to all the religious organizations and the Episcopal Church of St. Mark's was established in 1967.

CONTROVERSIAL CONCERNS

The Indians were worried about their traditional activities — in particular, hunting. Besides the ongoing effects of drainage and development in the Everglades, there were two tangible problems: tick eradication and the proposed National Park.

Cattle ranchers blamed deer for carrying the ticks which infected their free-ranging herds. In 1948 a scheme paid hunters to eradicate the deer however they could. Often the carcasses were just left to rot, only the ears being removed to turn in for cash.

Not only the Indians but genuine sportsmen protested. The first traditional Wild Hog Barbeque was held in 1950 near the Loop Road in the Big Cypress to raise awareness of the mass slaughter. Deaconess Bedell and the Friends of the Seminoles also took up the cause.

When the bounty hunters tried to kill deer on the Big Cypress Reservation, the Indians complained; the State of Florida had no jurisdiction in their territory and the scheme was faulty. It was decided that an independent study should be made and the National Audubon Society was contacted. The resulting report was that ticks are carried by most wild animals (raccoons, etc) and killing the deer would not solve the problem.

Finally, the tick eradication scheme was stopped and ranchers were forced to dip their cattle. Those animals that couldn't be corralled were shot instead. Incidentally, it was reported that the Indians were able to track and ambush wild steers, catching them by the horns and subduing them.

The formation of the Everglades National Park had its roots in the early 1900s. The Florida Federation of Women's Clubs had

Paradise Key near Homestead made into Royal Palm State Park in 1916 after the Florida East Coast Railway donated the land, thanks particularly to its vice-president J. E. Ingraham. In 1925 landscape architect Ernest F. Coe arrived in Miami and had a dream of saving the rest of the Everglades for posterity. After much persuading, Congress passed a bill in 1934 for the formation of the park but with a proviso that no money be spent for five years, mainly because recovery from the Depression was still taking up all available funds. Turmoil in Europe led to World War II and before long the United States was focusing on battle rather than conservation.

Again, the Indians were worried about the effect that a huge park, originally proposed to encompass two million acres, would have on their way of life. It was suggested that they could be official guides. Deaconess Bedell hoped that the Indians would be given as much consideration as the wildlife that would be preserved. She consulted with David Graham Copeland of the Collier Corporation which eventually donated a large parcel of the land. He was Chairman of the Boundary Committee for the park and assured the Deaconess that he was aware of her concerns for the Indians.

Eventually, only about one million acres was incorporated into the park, the rest of it being too expensive to buy from private landholders. Coe was upset that the Big Cypress lands could not be included because they ensured the flow of water into the Everglades.

On December 6, 1947, the grand opening of Everglades National Park was held in the town of Everglades and the Deaconess was invited to give the invocation. It was said that her time on the podium was longer than that of the guest of honor, Harry S Truman. After the ceremonies, she had a cordial lunch with the President and then rushed back to her Mission to sell souvenirs to all the visitors who had come into town.

In 1962 some of the Trail Indians were recognized as the Miccosukee Tribe and the National Park Service allowed them to remain on the strip of land along the Trail at Forty Mile Bend where they developed a cultural center.

The Deaconess is just visible walking away from the podium at the opening of Everglades National Park where President Truman was the guest of honor. *Photos Courtesy of Florida State Archives.*

Everglades National Park, December 6, 1947
Invocation
by Deaconess Harriet Bedell

Almighty God, Whose never-failing Providence ordereth all things in Heaven and earth, we praise Thee and thank Thee for Thy gifts of the wonders and beauties of nature – that Thou hast put it into the heart of man to preserve some of the beautiful places of the earth – beautiful birds, and animals, and rare plants – that through man's selfishness and commercial greed they may not become extinct.

Bless, we pray Thee, this park we are dedicating today. May it be a haven not only for the wild life, but where we may find the beauties and peace of nature – where we may go apart from the hurry and anxieties of this life.

We especially thank Thee for the approval and presence of our President, President Truman. May he have wisdom and strength to know and do Thy will.

Give grace and wisdom, we pray Thee, to those who are furthering the ideals of this park, that it may be a place of joy and pleasure.

May all who visit it be drawn nearer to God and get a glimpse of His peace and majesty amid the changing social order of the world to-day.

We ask all this through Him who brought peace and goodwill into the world at the first Christmas time, our Lord and Saviour Jesus Christ.

Amen.

RETIREMENT, 1960-1969

Hurricane Donna in 1960 is still talked about in the Everglades City area. The water rose so high in this sea-level town that residents crammed into the second floor of the courthouse for the duration. One story is that several youngsters swam over to the grocery store where they found the bread floating around inside.

The Deaconess was persuaded to go to Ochopee, away from the threat of a storm surge from the river, to stay with the tomato-farming Gaunt family. When she was able to return after the storm, the Mission House was a wreck. Water had damaged most of her belongings, soaking her books and papers in a bath of brackish water and silt.

Bishop Louttit instructed the manager of the Gray Inn, an Episcopal retirement home, to drive from Davenport in central Florida to collect her. The Deaconess rebuffed him; she wanted to check on her Indians. Fortunately, they lived on higher ground along the Trail and the traditional chickees stood up to the raging wind which blew through the open sides. But, the Deaconess stayed in the area to make sure the Indians got their share of relief supplies brought by the Red Cross and other welcome volunteers.

The Bishop promised a new missionary would take over Glade Cross and the Deaconess finally agreed to "retire" at the age of 85 but, even then, she did not stop being active. After moving to the William Crane Gray Inn for Older People, as the retirement home was officially called, she prepared Sunday School lessons and comforted other residents. She died on January 8, 1969, and was buried in Haines City.

Fortunately, collections of her papers reside at Harvard, the Smithsonian, and the Historical Museum of South Florida. Digital copies of 126 of her photos are online at the Florida State Archives. She had contributed to Episcopal publications all her missionary life and had issued mimeographed newsletters from the Glade Cross so we have documented records of her work and thoughts.

There was no new missionary and the Mission House was sold, repaired, and extended. It is still recognizable.

Her friend and neighbor Inez Magill commented, "The Seminoles never had a better friend than the Deaconess, and many of them moved away after the mission closed."[1]

Dr James L. Glenn, Indian Agent and local pastor, said in an interview in 1978, "She had about as much courage as any woman I ever saw".[2]

Tebeau, the authority on Collier County history, wrote while the Deaconess was still alive:[3]

> She is more a social worker than a crusading evangelist. Measured in terms of the number of lives she has touched and brightened, the achievements of the Deaconess Bedell assume monumental proportions.
>
> Deaconess Harriet Bedell is the Glade Cross Mission; and whatever usefulness and character it has is the stamp of her own personality upon it. She probably fits into no simple category of missionaries that her church knows. She has always been a pioneer; and she has been at home in Collier County which proudly calls her its own.
>
> This humble woman of God and servant of all who come to her ... gives one the impression she might go on forever, as indeed her spirit will.

---

[1] Magill, *From Ticks to Politics*, p.71.

[2] *Interview with James L. Glenn*, Southeastern Indian Oral History Project, University of Florida, http://www.uflib.ufl.edu/ufdc/.

[3] Tebeau, *Florida's Last Frontier*, pp. 80-82.

RECOGNITION

St Mark's Church on Marco Island has a Bedell chapel with a glorious Everglades mural and a new altar. It also has a cross belonging to the Deaconess which was used at the Glade Cross Mission.

In 2000 Harriet Bedell was made a Great Floridian by the state and her plaque hangs on the outside of the Museum of the Everglades, the old laundry building in Everglades City. Inside the Museum there is a display case dedicated to her.

In 2003 the following Resolution, originated by St. Stephen's Church, Coconut Grove, Florida, was passed by the Diocese of Southeast Florida and the Diocese of Alaska.

> WHEREAS Deaconess Harriet Bedell worked to bring the faith of Christ to the Cheyenne, Athabaskan, and Miccosukee Indian tribes and
> WHEREAS Deaconess Harriet Bedell sacrificed the opportunity to have her own family to work for the family of Christ in the new family she found with the Native Americans and
> WHEREAS Deaconess Harriet Bedell was not only accepted into the Native American way of life, but was also made a member of all three tribes by the elders because of her work and
> WHEREAS Deaconess Harriet Bedell decided to continue her work with the Miccosukee tribe even after her forced retirement and
> WHEREAS Deaconess Harriet Bedell brought the word of God to the Native Americans not only in her church worship but also through her school teaching and in her nursing and
> WHEREAS Deaconess Harriet Bedell was a driving force in the mission work not only in the Everglades but also in new missions along the Tamiami Trail and
> WHEREAS Deaconess Harriet Bedell has been recognized not only in the histories of the Diocese of Oklahoma, the Diocese of Alaska, and the Dioceses of Southeast and Southwest Florida, but was invited to give the invocation at the opening of Everglades National Park with President Harry Truman and was recognized by the State of Florida as a Great Floridian in 2000;

THEREFORE BE IT RESOLVED that the Diocese of Southeast Florida set aside the 8th of January on the Diocesan calendar to be marked as the feast day for Deaconess Harriet Bedell and

BE IT FURTHER RESOLVED that the Diocese of Southeast Florida present a resolution to the General Convention of 2006 that Deaconess Harriet Bedell be added to the calendar of saints and included in Lesser Feasts and Fasts and that the 8th of January be set aside on the calendar of saints to commemorate her.

The commemoration for her is:

Holy God, you chose your faithful servant Harriett Bedell to exercise the ministry of deaconess and to be a missionary among indigenous peoples. Fill us with compassion and respect for all people, empowering us for the work of ministry throughout the world, through Jesus Christ our Lord, who lives and reigns with you and the Holy Spirit, one God, for ever and ever. *Amen*

The resolution was passed for a trial period at the 2006 General Convention and was approved in 2009.

Great Floridians 2000 plaque at the Museum of the Everglades, Everglades City. *Photo by the author.*

Artist Hannah Ineson in front of the Everglades mural she painted in the Bedell Chapel at St Mark's Episcopal Church on Marco Island.
Photo Courtesy of Patricia Huff.

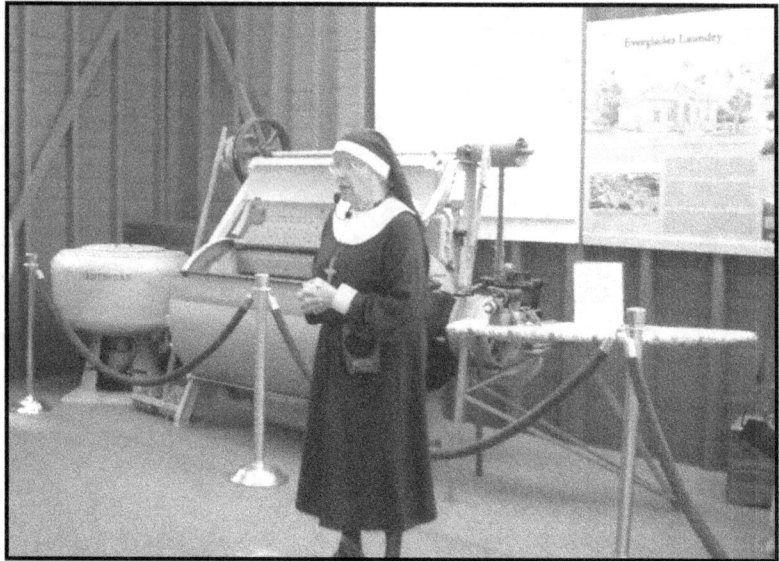

Marion Nicolay of the Marco Island Historical Society giving a presentation about the Deaconess at the Museum of the Everglades in March, 2009. *Photo by the author.*

The late Carol Moseman of the Friends of the Museum of the Everglades with members of the Seminole Tribe on a prize-winning float in the Independence Day Parade in Everglades City, July, 2005. *Photo by the author.*

APPENDIX. BRIEF BIOGRAPHIES

Barron Gift Collier (1873-1939)
Collier was born in Memphis, TN, and began his streetcar advertising business as a teenager. By the time he was in his early twenties, he had amassed a fortune and moved to New York where he became a prominent citizen. He advocated the painting of lines down the middle of streets to control traffic and the formation of Interpol to promote cooperation among international police organizations. He was active in the Boy Scouts at national level and was an economic advisor to President Coolidge.

Collier first came to Florida in 1911 on a visit to Useppa island which he bought. He purchased almost a million acres of land in southwest Florida, much of which was incorporated into Collier County in 1923 with its seat in the town of Everglades. He was also active in Fort Myers and was the publisher of the *News-Press*. Collier was married to Juliet Carnes and had three sons (Miles, Samuel, and Barron, Jr) who took over his many commercial activities after his sudden death in 1939.

David Graham Copeland (1885-1949)
Copeland was born in Bamberg, SC, and educated at Rensselaer Polytechnic Institute and the Naval Academy in Annapolis. He served in the U.S. Navy during World War I as an engineer in large construction projects. In 1923 he was hired by Collier and moved to the village of Everglades to supervise the building of the town and the Tamiami Trail. He also managed many of Collier's commercial companies and was Chairman of the Board of County Commissioners until he was elected to the Florida House of Representatives in 1947.

Copeland was interested in history and accumulated over a 1000 pages of typed notes about the area which became the basis for Tebeau's book *Florida's Last Frontier*. Copeland died suddenly in 1949 while visiting his wife's family in New Orleans.

Bishop William Crane Gray (1835-1919)
Gray was born in Lambertville, NJ, but moved as a child to Tennessee where his father was a missionary priest in the Episcopal Church. While he attended Kenyon College he preached to small local communities. He was appointed to the parish of Bolivar, KY, in 1860 and moved to Nashville in 1880. When the Diocese of Florida split in 1892, he was made Bishop of the Missionary District of Southern Florida and traveled from his base in Orlando all over the territory. He took an active interest in the Glade Cross Mission to the Seminoles which the Church operated from 1894.

Gray retired in 1914 and lived with a son in Nashville until his death in 1919. A retirement home in Davenport, FL, was named after him in 1951; it was sold in 2004.

Deacon David Pendleton Oakerhater (1848?-1931)

Oakerhater was raised as a traditional Southern Cheyenne and took the name "Okuhhatuh" (Sun Dancer) after the warrior's shield that he designed. After several battles against white horse thieves and cattle rustlers, he was taken prisoner in 1875 and shipped to Fort Marion (Castillo de San Marcos) in St. Augustine, FL, where he was taught to speak, read, and write English by Lt. R. H. Pratt (who later issued a sympathetic report on the Florida Seminoles). In 1878 Oakerhater was sponsored by the Pendleton family to continue his education at an Episcopal school in Paris Hill, NY, where he was baptized and took the name "David Pendleton".

In 1881 Oakerhater was made a Deacon and was sent as a missionary to Cheyenne territory where he settled in 1898 at the Whirlwind Mission, northwest of Oklahoma City. The Mission was discontinued in 1915 and he was pensioned off. Oakerhater was married four times but only one of his children survived. He died in 1931 and was named a Saint by the 1985 Episcopal General Convention. His feast day is September 1. Some of his letters and an extensive biography are available in the Oklahoma State University Digital Library at their website: http://digital.library.okstate.edu/oakerhater/index.html.

Bishop Peter Trimble Rowe (1856-1942)

Rowe was born in Toronto, Canada, where he learned to cope with the cold and outdoor life. After graduating from Trinity College, Toronto, and being ordained as a minister in 1878, he served as a missionary to the Indians on Lake Huron. His next assignment in 1882 was at Sault Ste. Marie, Michigan, where he built up the congregation and established missions in the countryside. In 1895 he was elected Bishop of the new Alaska Missionary District and won the respect of gold rush prospectors, as well as the natives, with his hardy physical constitution and bravery in coping with the frozen conditions. He remained there actively working until his death in 1942.

SOURCES

The classic biography of Harriet Bedell is *A Woman Set Apart*, written by William and Ellen Hartley and published in 1963. A copy of the book in the Everglades Society for Historical Preservation Library is inscribed:

> *In appreciation for your interest.*
> *Harriet M. Bedell*
> *Deaconess*

The Hartleys left their collection of papers about the Deaconess to the Historical Museum of South Florida.

For ecclesiastical history in South Florida, Cushman's *The Sound of Bells* is the authoritative source and includes biographies of the bishops in the Diocese of South Florida.

For background history, see *Florida's Last Frontier; the History of Collier County* by Charlton W. Tebeau which covers the area from earliest times until the 1960s.

The Internet is an invaluable tool for researchers and, fortunately, many documents and pictures have now been digitized. The excellent www.floridamemory.com site, part of the Florida State Archives, has provided a majority of the photographs in this book.

BOOKS

Ames, Elizabeth Scott, **The Deaconess of the Everglades**. 1995: Cortland Press, Cortland, NY (Phil Fisher illustrations).

Barbour, Thomas, **That Vanishing Eden; A Naturalist's Florida**. 1944: Little, Brown and Company, Boston, MA (travels, arguments against drainage and development).

Carlin, Virginia, **I Remember Marco; A Tale of Two Villages**. 1996: Carlin Enterprises, Marco Island, FL (local history).

Coe, Charles H, **Red Patriots; The Story of the Seminoles**. 1974: University Presses of Florida, Gainesville, FL (reprint of 1898 book, Tebeau introduction).

Cushman, Jr, John D, **The Sound of Bells; The Episcopal Church in South Florida, 1892-1969**. 1976: University Presses of Florida, Gainesville, FL (history with biographies of 4 bishops, references).

Douglas, Marjory Stoneman, **The Everglades; River of Grass**. 1974: Mockingbird, Marietta, GA (first published in 1947, history of Glades, plea for conservation).

Downs, Dorothy, **Art of the Florida Seminole & Miccosukee Indians**. 1995: University Press of Florida, Gainesville, FL (details of clothing and crafts).

Fritz, Florence, **Unknown Florida** 1963: University of Miami Press, Coral Gables, FL (history of Southwest Florida).

Glenn, James Lafayette, **My Work Among the Florida Seminoles**. 1982: University Presses of Florida, Gainesville, FL (description of his work at the Dania Reservation, introduction and notes by Kersey).

Hartley, William & Ellen, **A Woman Set Apart**. 1963: Dodd, Mead & Company, New York, NY (definitive biography of Harriet Bedell).

Kersey, Harry A, **Pelts, Plumes, and Hides; White Traders among the Seminole Indians, 1870-1930**. 1975: University Presses of Florida, Gainsville, FL (includes Brown's Boat Landing, Storter, Smallwood).

Kersey, Harry A, **An Assumption of Sovereignty; Social and Political Transformation among the Florida Seminoles, 1953-1979**. 1996: University of Nebraska Press, Lincoln & London, NB (details of tribal dealings with state and federal government).

Magill, Inez, **From Ticks to Politics.** n/d: printed privately, Everglades City, FL (life in Everglades City during the 1950s when the author was Deputy County Clerk).

Neill, Wilfred T, **The Story of the Seminole Indians.** 1956: Great Outdoors Publishing Co., St. Petersburg, FL (small paperback with comments and photos).

Parkman, Mary R, **Heroes of To-Day.** 1917: The Century Co., New York, NY (chapter about Bishop Rowe of Alaska).

Peithman, Irvin M, **The Unconquered Seminole Indians.** 1957: Great Outdoors Publishing, St Petersburg, FL (large format, contemporary comments and photos).

Perdichizzi, Elizabeth McDonald, **Island Voices; They Came to Marco Island.** 2006: Caxambas Publishing, Marco Island, FL (local history).

Reynolds, Doris, **When Peacocks were Roasted and Mullet was Fried.** 1973: Enterprise Publishing, Naples, FL (local history with recipes).

Stuck, Hudson, **The Alaskan Missions of the Episcopal Church.** 1920: Domestic and Foreign Missionary Society, New York, NY (author was Archdeacon of the Yukon, knew Bedell).

Tebeau, Charlton W, **Florida's Last Frontier; The History of Collier County.** 1966: University of Miami Press, Coral Gables, FL (classic history of the area).

Tebeau, Charlton W, **Man in the Everglades.** 1968: University of Miami Press, Miami, FL (settlers and natives in the Everglades National Park area).

West, Patsy, **The Enduring Seminoles; From Alligator Wrestling to Ecotourism.** 1998: University Press of Florida, Gainesville, FL (social and economic history, good bibliography).

Wright, E. Lynne, **More Than Petticoats; Remarkable Florida Women.** 2001: Globe Pequot Press, Guilford, CT (brief biographies of pioneering women).

MAGAZINES

Brown, Percy, "A Family of Early Settlers of Immokalee". *Timepiece, v.XVI, n.1, 1989,* Collier County Historical Society, Naples, FL (reminiscences by grandson of Bill Brown who traded with Indians at the Landing near Immokalee).

Covington, James W, "Federal and State Relations with the Florida Seminoles, 1875-1901". *Tequesta #32, 1972,* Historical Museum of South Florida, Miami, FL.

Covington, James W, "Seminole Leadership: Changing Substance, 1858-1958". *Tequesta #40, 1980,* Historical Museum of South Florida, Miami, FL.

Covington, James W, "The State of Florida; The Florida Indians, 1954-1961". *Tequesta #46, 1986,* Historical Museum of South Florida, Miami, FL.

Davis, Hilda J, "The History of Seminole Clothing and Its Multi-Colored Designs". *American Anthropologist, NS v.57, n.5, 1955,* Blackwell Publishing (available online at www.jstor.org).

Hartley, William and Ellen, "White Sister of the Seminoles". *Coronet, August, v.46, n.4, 1959,* Esquire Inc, Chicago, IL.

Huntoon, George, "Memories & Tall Tales of Collier County". *Timepiece, v.XVI, n.1, 1989,* Collier County Historical Society, Naples, FL (reminiscences of Everglades City when Huntoon worked for Collier Corporation).

Kersey, Harry A, "The Friends of the Florida Seminoles Society: 1899-1926". *Tequesta #34, 1974,* Historical Museum of South Florida, Miami, FL.

Skinner, Alanson, "Notes on the Florida Seminole". *American Anthropologist, NS v.15, n.1, 1913,* Blackwell Publishing (available online at www.jstor.org).

West, Patricia, "Glade Cross Mission: An Influence on Florida Seminole Arts and Crafts". *American Indian Art Magazine, v.9, n.4, 1984,* Scottsdale, AZ.

South Florida in the late 1940s. *Picture Courtesy of Florida State Archives.*

TIME LINE

1857 Third Seminole War ended

1873 Barron Gift Collier born in Memphis, TN

1875 Harriet Bedell born in Buffalo, NY

1879 Pratt's Report on the Seminoles

1885 David Graham Copeland born in Bamberg, SC

1887 Lee County, FL, established

1891 WNIA started Immokalee mission

1892 William Crane Gray became Bishop of Missionary District of Southern Florida

1894 Harriet Bedell graduated from Normal School, started teaching

1895 Peter Trimble Rowe became Bishop of Alaska Missionary District

1898 Glade Cross Mission started by Bishop Gray

1898 David Pendleton Oakerhater went to new Whirlwind Mission

1906 Harriet Bedell attended Deaconess training school

1907 Harriet Bedell went to Whirlwind Mission, OK

1914 Glade Cross Mission closed; Bishop Gray retired

1916 Harriet Bedell went to Nenana, AK

1917 Harriet Bedell went to Stevens Village, AK

1922 Harriet Bedell made a Deaconess

1922 Missionary District of Southern Florida made a full Diocese led by Bishop Mann

1923 Collier County, FL, established

1928 Tamiami Trail in Collier County, FL, completed across the Everglades

1931 Harriet Bedell left Alaska

1933 Harriet Bedell opened Glade Cross Mission in town of Everglades, FL

1939 Barron Gift Collier died

1947 Everglades National Park officially opened on December 6th

1948 buildings in Caxambas on Marco Island, FL, moved to Goodland, FL

1949 David Graham Copeland died

1953 town of Everglades incorporated as a City

1960 Harriet Bedell forced to retire after Hurricane Donna

1969 Harriet Bedell died on January 8th

2006 Harriet Bedell's Feast Day on Church calendar

www.ingramcontent.com/pod-product-compliance
Lightning Source LLC
Chambersburg PA
CBHW072109290426
44110CB00014B/1879